DUSSELDORF TRAVEL GUIDE

Safe Traveler's Guides

COPYRIGHT

TABLE OF CONTENTS

1. WELCOME TO DÜSSELDORF

A Vibrant City Where Tradition Meets Innovation

Welcome to Düsseldorf – the cosmopolitan heart of western Germany. Situated along the banks of the Rhine River, Düsseldorf is a city that blends historic charm with cutting-edge modernity. From its lively Altstadt ("Old Town") and famous fashion scene to its thriving art culture and futuristic architecture, this city offers a dynamic experience for every kind of traveler.

Whether you're visiting for a long weekend or using Düsseldorf as a gateway to explore Germany and beyond, you'll find it to be a clean, safe, and welcoming city with a unique rhythm all its own.

Why Visit Düsseldorf?

Düsseldorf may not always top the list of European tourist hotspots, but it's a hidden gem packed with discoveries. Here are a few reasons why you'll fall in love with it:

- **A Walkable City with Great Public Transit:** Getting around is a breeze thanks to an excellent transport network and pedestrian-friendly neighborhoods.

- **Cultural Riches:** The city boasts more than 20 museums and galleries, world-class opera and symphony venues, and a vibrant street art scene.

- **The Altbier Experience:** Düsseldorf is home to a beer tradition unlike any other. Taste locally brewed *Altbier* in traditional pubs that haven't changed in centuries.

- **Shopping & Fashion Capital:** Known as one of Germany's fashion hubs, the upscale Königsallee and trendy boutiques in districts like Flingern are a shopper's paradise.

- **Green Spaces & River Views:** Enjoy picturesque riverside promenades, sprawling urban parks, and plenty of outdoor cafes and beer gardens.

- **Gateway to the Rhine-Ruhr Region:** Düsseldorf's central location makes it an ideal base for day trips to nearby cities like Cologne, Essen, and Wuppertal.

Quick Facts About Düsseldorf

- **Location:** North Rhine-Westphalia (Nordrhein-Westfalen), Western Germany

- **Population:** Approximately 640,000

- **Language:** German (though English is widely understood in hotels, restaurants, and tourist areas)

- **Currency:** Euro (€)

- **Time Zone:** Central European Time (CET) / Central European Summer Time (CEST)

- **International Airport:** Düsseldorf International Airport (DUS), just 15 minutes from the city center

- **Famous For:** Altbier, Königsallee, fashion fairs, the Rhine promenade, and being a center for art and culture

A City with a Story

Founded as a small fishing village in the 12th century, Düsseldorf has evolved into a global city known for its international trade fairs, vibrant expat community, and high quality of life. Though heavily damaged during World War II, the city has reinvented itself, rising from the ashes with innovative urban planning and bold architectural landmarks—especially in areas like the MedienHafen.

Yet, for all its modern energy, Düsseldorf retains a strong connection to its traditions. This duality is visible everywhere—from medieval churches nestled beside glass skyscrapers to local festivals like *Karneval*, where the entire city lets loose in colorful celebration.

Who Will Enjoy Düsseldorf?

Düsseldorf is ideal for:

- **Culture lovers** seeking world-class art and classical music

- **Foodies** interested in German specialties and international fusion cuisine

- **Solo travelers** looking for a safe, easy-to-navigate city

- **Couples** seeking romantic strolls by the Rhine and candlelit dinners

- **Families** looking for green parks, fun museums, and river cruises

- **Business travelers** attending trade fairs, with plenty of downtime options

Get Ready to Explore

This guide will take you through everything you need to know to make the most of your time in Düsseldorf—from planning and practical tips to hidden gems and local favorites. Whether it's your first visit or your fifth, Düsseldorf has a way of surprising you with its balance of sophistication and down-to-earth hospitality.

Pack your walking shoes, bring your curiosity, and get ready to discover a side of Germany that's often overlooked—but unforgettable.

2. PLANNING YOUR TRIP

Best Time to Visit

Düsseldorf is a year-round destination, but the best time to visit depends on your interests:

- **Spring (March–May):** Mild temperatures, blooming parks, and fewer tourists. Great for walking tours and day trips.

- **Summer (June–August):** Warm weather, long days, and open-air festivals. Expect larger crowds and higher hotel rates.

- **Autumn (September–November):** Crisp air, colorful foliage, and fewer tourists. A perfect season for photography and museums.

- **Winter (December–February):** Cold but charming, especially during the

Christmas Market season. Don't miss the magical atmosphere in the Altstadt.

Special Event Alert: Düsseldorf's *Karneval* (Carnival), held in February or early March, is one of the biggest celebrations in Germany. Book well in advance if traveling during this period.

Entry Requirements & Visas

- **EU/EEA Citizens:** No visa required. Just bring a valid ID card or passport.

- **U.S., Canada, Australia, UK:** Visa-free for stays up to 90 days within a 180-day period (Schengen Zone rules apply).

- **Other Nationalities:** Check the "German Federal Foreign Office" or your local consulate for specific visa requirements.

Tip: Always ensure your passport is valid for at least three months beyond your planned departure from the Schengen Area.

Health & Safety Tips

- **Healthcare:** Germany has excellent healthcare. EU citizens can use their European Health Insurance Card (EHIC), while others should have travel insurance covering medical care.

- **Pharmacies (Apotheken):** Widely available and easily identifiable by a red "A" sign. Most staff speak some English.

- **Vaccinations:** No special vaccinations are required to enter Germany.

- **Drinking Water:** Safe and high-quality tap water throughout the city.

Travel Insurance & Emergency Contacts

Travel Insurance: Strongly recommended to cover medical expenses, cancellations, and lost items.

Emergency Numbers in Germany:

- **Police:** 110

- **Fire & Ambulance:** 112

- **Medical Emergency (non-urgent):** 116 117

Keep your insurance provider's number and embassy contact info handy.

Budgeting & Currency Exchange

- **Currency:** Euro (€)

- **Average Daily Budget (Mid-range):** €100–€150

    o Hotel: €60–€120

    o Meals: €25–€40

    o Transport & Tickets: €10–€20

ATMs & Cards:

- ATMs (Geldautomaten) are widely available.

- Credit and debit cards are accepted, but some smaller businesses may prefer cash.

Tipping Etiquette:

- Round up or add ~5–10% in restaurants.

- Cash is preferred for tips, even if you pay by card.

Public Holidays & Local Customs

Key Public Holidays in Düsseldorf:

- **New Year's Day (Jan 1)**

- **Good Friday & Easter Monday**

- **Labour Day (May 1)**

- **Ascension Day (varies)**

- **German Unity Day (Oct 3)**

- **Christmas (Dec 25–26)**

Shops and many businesses are closed on public holidays, including Sundays.

Local Customs & Behavior:

- Be punctual—Germans value timeliness.

- Use polite greetings (*Guten Tag*, *Danke*, *Bitte*).

- Recycle and respect clean public spaces.

- Smoking is restricted indoors and near transport hubs.

Final Tips

- **Language:** While many locals speak English, learning a few German phrases will go a long way.

- **Wi-Fi:** Widely available in hotels and cafes. Consider a local SIM or eSIM for constant access.

- **Apps to Download:**

  - **DB Navigator:** Train and transit schedules

  - **Google Maps or Citymapper:** Navigation

  - **Too Good To Go:** Cheap leftover food from local cafes

  - **Eventim:** Concert and event tickets

Düsseldorf is well-equipped for international visitors and offers a hassle-free experience from arrival to departure. With your trip carefully planned, you're ready to explore the next part of the journey: **getting around and choosing the perfect place to stay—** covered in the chapters ahead.

3. GETTING THERE & AROUND

Düsseldorf is one of Germany's most accessible cities, both in terms of international connectivity and ease of getting around once you arrive. Whether you're flying in, arriving by train, or exploring the city's neighborhoods on foot or by bike, Düsseldorf offers a wide range of efficient and traveler-friendly options. This chapter will guide you through the best ways to arrive and move around the city with confidence.

Arriving in Düsseldorf: Airports & Train Stations

Düsseldorf International Airport (DUS)

Düsseldorf International Airport is the third-largest in Germany and a major hub for both domestic and international flights. Located just 9 kilometers (about 5.5 miles) from the city center, it offers a smooth transition from air travel to urban exploration.

Transport from the Airport:

- **S-Bahn (S11):** Connects the airport to Düsseldorf Hauptbahnhof (Central Station) in about 15 minutes.

- **Regional Trains:** Depart from the Düsseldorf Flughafen train station, accessible via the SkyTrain monorail within the airport complex.

- **Taxis:** Readily available outside the terminals; the fare to the city center typically ranges from €25 to €30.

- **Rideshare Services:** Uber and Free Now operate in Düsseldorf.

- **Car Rentals:** All major rental agencies are located in the terminal complex.

Düsseldorf Hauptbahnhof (Central Station)

Düsseldorf Hauptbahnhof is the city's main rail hub and one of the busiest in Germany. It offers high-speed ICE trains to cities like Cologne, Frankfurt, Berlin, Amsterdam, and Brussels, as well as frequent regional and local connections.

The station is centrally located and well-served by U-Bahn, S-Bahn, trams, and buses, making it an ideal arrival point for those traveling within Europe.

Public Transportation: S-Bahn, U-Bahn, Trams, Buses

Düsseldorf has a modern, integrated public transport system operated by **Rheinbahn**, covering the entire city and surrounding areas. All modes use a unified ticketing system.

U-Bahn (Subway)

The U-Bahn operates both underground and overground, providing rapid transit within the city. It's the fastest option for longer inner-city routes.

S-Bahn (Suburban Trains)

The S-Bahn connects Düsseldorf with surrounding towns and cities in the Rhine-Ruhr metropolitan region. Line S11 is particularly useful for reaching the airport.

Trams (Straßenbahn)

Trams are convenient for short- to mid-range travel within Düsseldorf and offer scenic routes through historic and modern districts.

Buses

Buses fill in the gaps of the U-Bahn and tram networks, reaching residential neighborhoods and operating during off-hours when other systems run less frequently.

Tickets & Fares:

- Tickets can be purchased at station machines, via the Rheinbahn app, or from kiosks.

- Options include single tickets, day passes, and multi-day tourist cards (e.g., DüsseldorfCard).

- Tickets must be validated before boarding unless bought digitally.

A single short-distance fare starts at around €3.10, and a day pass is typically around €7.60.

Cycling & Walking Routes

Düsseldorf is a compact, bike-friendly city with an expanding network of dedicated cycling lanes. Many locals use bikes for commuting and leisure, and visitors can do the same with ease.

Bike Rentals

- **Nextbike** and **Lime** offer bike-sharing options throughout the city.

- Rental bikes can be picked up and dropped off at various docking stations or parked responsibly in permitted areas.

Popular Cycling Routes

- **Rhine Embankment Promenade:** A scenic path ideal for leisure rides.

- **Nordpark to Hofgarten:** A green route connecting two of the city's most beautiful parks.

- **MedienHafen Loop:** Great for architecture and riverside views.

Walking

The central districts of Düsseldorf, particularly the Altstadt, Carlstadt, and Königsallee areas, are ideal for walking. The city's flat terrain and clean streets make it perfect for leisurely strolls and spontaneous detours.

Car Rentals & Driving Tips

While not necessary for most city visitors, renting a car may be useful for those planning regional excursions.

Car Rentals

Available at the airport, central train station, and in various city locations. Major providers include Sixt, Europcar, Hertz, and Avis.

Driving in Düsseldorf

- **Road Rules:** Drive on the right-hand side. Seat belts are mandatory. Using a mobile phone without a hands-free device is illegal.

- **Speed Limits:** Generally 50 km/h in cities and up to 130 km/h on the autobahn (some sections have no limit).

- **Parking:** Street parking is limited in the city center, but public parking garages are widely available.

- **Environmental Zone:** Düsseldorf has a low-emission zone (Umweltzone). Cars must display a green emissions sticker (Feinstaubplakette) to enter. Most rental cars are compliant.

Accessibility Information

Düsseldorf is among Germany's more accessible cities and is continually improving infrastructure for travelers with disabilities.

Public Transportation

- Most S-Bahn, U-Bahn, and tram stations are equipped with elevators or ramps.

- Newer vehicles are designed for low-floor, step-free access.

- Real-time updates on elevator availability are provided on the Rheinbahn website and app.

Attractions & Facilities

- Major museums, theaters, shopping centers, and hotels provide wheelchair access.

- Public restrooms with accessible features are available in central locations, particularly near tourist areas and transport hubs.

Tip: Travelers requiring assistance should contact attractions or transport providers in advance to confirm accessibility options.

Düsseldorf combines efficiency with comfort, offering multiple ways to explore the city without hassle. Whether you choose to bike along the Rhine, ride the tram to the Altstadt, or simply stroll through leafy boulevards, getting around is part of the pleasure of visiting this dynamic and well-connected city.

4. WHERE TO STAY

Düsseldorf offers a diverse range of accommodations for every type of traveler, whether you're seeking luxury, creativity, charm, or affordability. Choosing the right place to stay depends largely on what you want to experience during your visit. From riverside views and bustling nightlife to artistic enclaves and upscale shopping, each neighborhood offers a distinct atmosphere.

Top Neighborhoods

Altstadt (Old Town)

Often called "the longest bar in the world," the Altstadt is the historic heart of Düsseldorf. It's lively, centrally located, and perfect for nightlife, sightseeing, and access to major landmarks.

- Best for: First-time visitors, nightlife, historic charm

- Pros: Walkable, well-connected by public transport, full of restaurants, bars, and museums

- Cons: Can be noisy, especially at night

MedienHafen (Media Harbor)

A modern district transformed from an industrial port into an architectural showcase, MedienHafen is known for its cutting-edge buildings and stylish atmosphere.

- Best for: Architecture lovers, business travelers, modern aesthetics

- Pros: Scenic waterfront, trendy bars and restaurants, close to the Rhine

- Cons: Less central, quieter at night

Flingern

Located east of the city center, Flingern is a hip, up-and-coming area popular with artists, students, and young professionals. It offers a mix of independent shops, cafes, galleries, and street art.

- Best for: Creative travelers, budget-conscious visitors, local experiences

- Pros: Artistic vibe, affordable accommodation, great food scene

- Cons: Not as polished, a bit farther from major tourist sites

Oberkassel

On the opposite side of the Rhine, Oberkassel is a leafy, residential neighborhood known for its elegant architecture and relaxed lifestyle. It offers a more local experience.

- Best for: Families, long-term stays, quieter ambiance

- Pros: Beautiful homes, great for riverside walks, local markets

- Cons: Less nightlife, slightly less convenient for short stays

Accommodation Options

Düsseldorf caters to all types of travelers, from solo backpackers to luxury seekers. Here are the main categories of accommodation available:

Hotels

Hotels range from international chains to boutique options. Many are located near the Hauptbahnhof, Altstadt, and Königsallee.

- **Business Hotels:** Often found near the Messe (trade fair area) and airport. Equipped with conference facilities.

- **Luxury Hotels:** Concentrated around Königsallee and the Rhine.

- **Boutique Hotels:** Scattered across Altstadt, MedienHafen, and Flingern for a more personalized experience.

Hostels

Ideal for budget travelers, hostels offer dormitory beds, shared kitchens, and often a social atmosphere.

- Most are centrally located near the Hauptbahnhof or Altstadt.

- Popular options include backpacker hostels, youth hostels, and design-oriented budget stays.

Bed & Breakfasts (B&Bs)

More intimate than hotels, B&Bs are often family-run and provide a local touch. They are available in quieter neighborhoods like Oberkassel or Flingern.

Short-Term Rentals

Apartments and studios are widely available through platforms like Airbnb. These are perfect for travelers wanting more space, kitchen facilities, or a home-like environment.

- Great for families, remote workers, or longer stays.

- Be aware of local regulations and minimum night requirements, especially during trade fairs.

Recommended Stays for Different Budgets

Luxury (Over €200/night)

- **Breidenbacher Hof** (Altstadt): Iconic 5-star hotel with opulent interiors and top-tier service.

- **Hyatt Regency Düsseldorf** (MedienHafen): Modern luxury with panoramic river views and spa facilities.

- **Hotel Kö59 Düsseldorf – by Hyatt** (Königsallee): Elegant, centrally located hotel ideal for shopping trips.

Mid-Range (€80–€200/night)

- **25hours Hotel Das Tour** (Pempelfort): Stylish and artistic, with rooftop views and a quirky French restaurant.

- **me and all hotel düsseldorf** (Stadtmitte): Urban boutique hotel with co-working space and a local vibe.

- **Motel One Düsseldorf-Hauptbahnhof**: Affordable, design-focused chain with great comfort and central location.

Budget (Under €80/night)

- **Backpackers Düsseldorf** (Friedrichstadt): Friendly, well-kept hostel with kitchen facilities.

- **a&o Düsseldorf Hauptbahnhof**: Basic but reliable, offering both private and dorm rooms.

- **Hotel Windsor** (Flingern): Family-run, budget-friendly with excellent public transport access.

Düsseldorf's variety of neighborhoods and accommodation styles ensures every visitor can find a home base that matches their interests, comfort level, and budget. Whether you want to stay in the heart of the action or retreat to a peaceful corner of the city, the right lodging will enhance your experience.

5. TOP ATTRACTIONS

Düsseldorf is a city that seamlessly blends historic charm with modern innovation. Its compact size makes it easy to explore, yet it offers a rich variety of sights that appeal to history enthusiasts, art lovers, architecture admirers, and casual travelers alike. This chapter highlights Düsseldorf's most iconic and culturally significant attractions.

Altstadt (Old Town) & "The Longest Bar in the World"

Düsseldorf's Altstadt is more than just the historic heart of the city—it's a living, breathing cultural hub. Though covering less than half a square kilometer, this "Old Town" is densely packed with cobblestone streets, centuries-old churches, and over 250 bars, pubs, and breweries. Locals affectionately refer to it as *"the longest bar in the world,"* because you can practically go bar-hopping without ever leaving the block.

Highlights include:

- **St. Lambertus Church:** A striking church with a twisted spire, rebuilt after World War II but preserving its medieval roots.

- **Brauereien (Breweries):** Try a glass of traditional Altbier—dark, top-fermented, and locally brewed—at historic venues like Uerige, Füchschen, or Schlüssel.

- **Burgplatz:** A scenic square along the Rhine with views of the river and the old castle tower, now housing the city's Maritime Museum.

This area is ideal for strolling, people-watching, and immersing yourself in Düsseldorf's social and culinary culture.

Rhine Embankment Promenade (Rheinuferpromenade)

Stretching along the banks of the Rhine River, the Rheinuferpromenade connects the Old Town to the MedienHafen district in a wide, tree-lined walkway ideal for pedestrians and cyclists.

What makes this promenade special:

- It was built above a highway that now runs underground, freeing up surface space for public enjoyment.

- Lively and elegant, it features cafes, restaurants, public art, and river cruise docks.

- A perfect place to watch the sunset over the Rhine or join locals for a weekend stroll.

On warm days, the promenade becomes a social boulevard, buzzing with street musicians, skaters, and families enjoying the fresh air and river views.

Königsallee (Luxury Shopping Boulevard)

Nicknamed *"Kö,"* Königsallee is one of Germany's most prestigious shopping streets. Divided by a landscaped canal and flanked by chestnut trees, the boulevard combines luxury retail with scenic beauty.

Key features:

- Designer boutiques from brands such as Chanel, Gucci, Louis Vuitton, and Prada.

- Elegant arcades and upscale department stores like Galeria Kaufhof and Breuninger.

- Art galleries, luxury hotels, and fine dining just steps away.

Even if high-end shopping is not on your itinerary, walking along the Kö is a quintessential Düsseldorf experience, offering a glimpse into the city's polished and stylish character.

MedienHafen & Modern Architecture

Once a forgotten port area, the MedienHafen (Media Harbor) has been transformed into a vibrant district of modern architecture, creative businesses, and trendy restaurants.

Architectural highlights include:

- **Frank Gehry's Neuer Zollhof:** A trio of deconstructed buildings with reflective, curved facades that have become symbols of modern Düsseldorf.

- **Colorium:** A striking multicolored glass building designed by British architect William Alsop.

- **Rheinturm and bridges:** Visible from nearly every point in the harbor, anchoring the space with dramatic views.

Today, the district houses media companies, design firms, and upscale dining spots with views over the marina and river. It's especially photogenic at dusk when the city lights begin to reflect off the water and the buildings.

Rhine Tower (Rheinturm) & Observation Deck

Standing at 240.5 meters, the Rheinturm is Düsseldorf's tallest structure and one of its most recognizable landmarks. It was built in the late 1970s as a telecommunications tower and now doubles as a visitor attraction.

Key features:

- **Observation Deck (168 meters):** Offers panoramic views of the city, Rhine River, and surrounding countryside. On clear days, you can see as far as Cologne Cathedral.

- **Revolving Restaurant:** Named *QOMO*, it completes a full rotation every 72 minutes, offering fine dining with a view.

- **Light Sculpture Clock:** The vertical light strip on the side of the tower is actually the world's largest digital clock, designed by artist Horst H. Baumann.

The tower is a must-visit for orientation, photography, and appreciating Düsseldorf's cityscape from above.

Benrath Palace & Park (Schloss Benrath)

Located in the southern district of Benrath, this 18th-century Baroque palace is one of the most elegant and well-preserved in North Rhine-Westphalia.

What to see:

- **The Palace:** Built between 1755 and 1770 as a summer residence for Elector Palatine Charles Theodor. The architecture is an excellent example of late Rococo style.

- **Gardens and Parklands:** Spanning over 60 hectares, the grounds include formal French gardens, English landscape sections, and forested trails.

- **Museums:** The main building houses the Museum of European Garden Art, while auxiliary buildings feature exhibitions on natural history and palace life.

Benrath Palace offers a peaceful escape from the city's hustle and is ideal for architecture and history enthusiasts.

Hofgarten (City Courtyard Gardens)

Düsseldorf's oldest and most central park, Hofgarten stretches from the Altstadt to the Tonhalle concert hall, offering a blend of natural beauty and artistic flair.

Why visit:

- **Landscape Design:** Inspired by English gardens with winding paths, ponds, and bridges.

- **Sculptures and Monuments:** Featuring works by famous artists including Johann Peter Melchior and Ewald Mataré.

- **Surrounding Institutions:** The park is bordered by cultural landmarks such as the Kunstpalast (art museum) and the NRW-Forum.

It's a serene spot for a picnic, a morning jog, or simply a quiet pause amid your sightseeing.

Eko-Haus of Japanese Culture

Düsseldorf is home to one of Europe's largest Japanese communities, and the Eko-Haus serves as a cultural bridge between Japan and Germany.

Attractions include:

- **Traditional Japanese Temple:** One of the few authentic Japanese Buddhist temples in Europe.

- **Japanese Garden:** Meticulously landscaped with koi ponds, stone lanterns, and bonsai trees.

- **Cultural Center:** Hosts exhibitions, concerts, language classes, and tea ceremonies.

Located in the Niederkassel district, Eko-Haus is a peaceful and educational experience that reflects the city's international spirit.

Kaiserswerth Historic District

Kaiserswerth, once an independent medieval town, is now a charming neighborhood in Düsseldorf's northern outskirts. It is rich in history and character.

What to explore:

- **Imperial Palace Ruins (Kaiserpfalz):** The remains of Emperor Barbarossa's 12th-century fortress overlook the Rhine and are open to the public.

- **Baroque Houses and Cobblestone Streets:** The town center retains its historic architecture and tranquil charm.

- **Florence Nightingale Connection:** Kaiserswerth was the location of the deaconess hospital where Nightingale studied nursing.

Kaiserswerth is easily reached by tram and offers a quieter, more reflective slice of Düsseldorf's history.

Düsseldorf's top attractions are a reflection of its identity—historic yet forward-looking, elegant but accessible, full of art, energy, and surprises. Whether you're gazing at the skyline from the Rheinturm, sipping Altbier in the Old Town, or discovering Japanese tranquility in Niederkassel, the city's diversity ensures every traveler will find something unforgettable.

6. MUSEUMS & CULTURAL HIGHLIGHTS

Düsseldorf is not only a city of business and fashion, but also one of Germany's most vibrant cultural hubs. It boasts a rich artistic tradition, a strong connection to avant-garde movements, and a dynamic museum landscape that reflects both historical depth and contemporary creativity. Whether you're a devoted art lover, curious about cinema, or traveling with children, Düsseldorf offers cultural experiences for every interest.

Kunstsammlung Nordrhein-Westfalen (K20, K21, Schmela Haus)

The Kunstsammlung Nordrhein-Westfalen is the leading modern and contemporary art museum in the city, spread across three venues: **K20**, **K21**, and the **Schmela Haus**.

Together, they form one of the most important collections of 20th and 21st-century art in Germany.

K20 (Grabbeplatz)

Housed in a striking black granite building in the city center, K20 focuses on modern art from the early 20th century.

- Highlights include works by **Paul Klee**, **Pablo Picasso**, **Henri Matisse**, **Piet Mondrian**, and **Wassily Kandinsky**.

- Post-war American artists such as **Jackson Pollock**, **Andy Warhol**, and **Mark Rothko** are also prominently featured.

- The building itself is architecturally significant, blending elegance with a sense of spacious openness.

K21 (Ständehaus)

Located in a former Prussian parliament building near the southern edge of the

Hofgarten, K21 is dedicated to contemporary art.

- The grand glass dome covers a network of steel walkways suspended in the air, part of the interactive installation "**in orbit**" by artist **Tomás Saraceno**, which visitors can walk through (advance booking and appropriate footwear required).

- The collection features international contemporary artists such as **Marina Abramović**, **Thomas Schütte**, and **Cindy Sherman**.

- K21 often hosts thought-provoking temporary exhibitions and media installations.

Schmela Haus

Located in the Flingern district, this smaller venue serves as a space for talks, lectures, and experimental exhibits. It was the first purpose-built private gallery in post-war

Germany, designed by Dutch architect Aldo van Eyck.

Museum Kunstpalast

Nestled along the Rhine and adjacent to the Ehrenhof cultural complex, the **Museum Kunstpalast** offers one of Düsseldorf's most diverse art collections. It spans several centuries and includes European painting, sculpture, applied arts, and graphic works.

- The museum's fine art collection ranges from the **Middle Ages to the Baroque period**, with masterpieces by **Peter Paul Rubens** and **Luca Giordano**.

- Its graphic arts collection is one of the most significant in Germany, featuring over 100,000 prints and drawings.

- The museum also includes **glass art**, contemporary photography, and design pieces, making it one of the city's most comprehensive art institutions.

- Regular temporary exhibitions feature international artists and attract art enthusiasts from all over Europe.

Fun fact: The museum is also home to the **Robert-Schumann-Saal**, a concert hall named after the composer who spent time in Düsseldorf during his career.

Goethe Museum

Located in the **Schloss Jägerhof**, a Rococo-style palace in the Hofgarten, the Goethe Museum is dedicated to the life and work of Germany's most celebrated writer, **Johann Wolfgang von Goethe**.

- The museum houses manuscripts, first editions, portraits, and personal items relating to Goethe's life.

- Though Goethe never lived in Düsseldorf, the museum explores his connections to the Rhineland and his enduring influence on German culture and intellectual life.

- Visitors can also learn about the **Sturm und Drang** and **Weimar Classicism** literary movements, in which Goethe played a central role.

- The setting—an 18th-century hunting lodge surrounded by gardens—adds charm and historical atmosphere to the experience.

It's a quieter but enriching stop for those interested in German literature, philosophy, and Enlightenment-era culture.

Film Museum

Located just off Burgplatz in the Altstadt, the **Düsseldorf Film Museum** is a must-visit for cinema lovers. It offers a fascinating look at the history of filmmaking from its earliest days to the digital era.

- Exhibits include vintage cameras, lighting equipment, film reels, costumes, and props from both German and international cinema.

- The museum features a **replica movie studio**, allowing visitors to step into a simulated set and understand the film production process.

- A special section is devoted to **German silent film pioneers**, including directors like F.W. Murnau and Fritz Lang.

- The museum also hosts film screenings at its in-house **Black Box cinema**, which shows classics, arthouse films, and international features in their original language.

The Film Museum blends nostalgia, education, and hands-on interaction, making it a favorite for both casual visitors and serious film buffs.

Aquazoo Löbbecke Museum

Located in the Nordpark district, the **Aquazoo Löbbecke Museum** is a unique hybrid of aquarium, natural history museum, and zoological exhibition. It is particularly popular with families and school groups.

- Home to over **500 animal species**, the Aquazoo showcases aquatic ecosystems from around the world, including tropical fish, sharks, amphibians, and reptiles.

- The museum also features taxidermied animals, dioramas, and educational displays that explain evolution, biodiversity, and environmental conservation.

- Its namesake, **Theodor Löbbecke**, was a 19th-century pharmacist and collector who laid the foundations for the museum's extensive shell and mollusk collections.

- Interactive exhibits and child-friendly displays make this one of Düsseldorf's top family attractions.

The Aquazoo is situated within **Nordpark**, which also offers beautiful Japanese gardens and fountains—perfect for a post-visit stroll.

From world-class modern art at K20 and K21 to historical insight at the Goethe Museum and interactive fun at the Aquazoo, Düsseldorf's cultural institutions reflect the city's multifaceted identity. Each museum not only preserves and presents knowledge but also offers a deeper appreciation of Düsseldorf's role as a creative capital in Germany and Europe.

7. ARTS, MUSIC & PERFORMANCE

Düsseldorf has long been a city of culture and creativity. With a rich musical tradition, a vibrant performing arts scene, and an eclectic mix of classical institutions and independent spaces, it offers both highbrow refinement and cutting-edge experimentation. Whether you're in the mood for grand opera, avant-garde theatre, or an open-air music festival, Düsseldorf has something for every taste.

Düsseldorf Opera House (Deutsche Oper am Rhein)

The **Deutsche Oper am Rhein** is one of Germany's most prestigious opera companies, with a shared ensemble performing in both Düsseldorf and Duisburg. Its Düsseldorf venue, located on Heinrich-Heine-Allee, is an elegant mid-20th century building that hosts a rich calendar of performances throughout the year.

- The repertoire ranges from **classic operas** by Mozart, Verdi, and Wagner to **contemporary works** and innovative reinterpretations.

- The house is also home to the **Ballett am Rhein**, directed by internationally renowned choreographer **Demis Volpi**, offering world-class ballet productions that combine tradition with modernity.

- With over 260 performances annually, the opera company is a cultural cornerstone in the Rhineland and consistently earns praise for its artistic excellence and accessibility.

Interesting fact: The building survived the destruction of World War II and was one of the first major cultural venues rebuilt in the post-war years, becoming a symbol of the city's resilience and renewal.

Tonhalle Düsseldorf (Concert Hall)

Housed in a former planetarium, the **Tonhalle** is one of Düsseldorf's most iconic venues for classical music. Its distinctive green dome makes it an architectural landmark along the Rhine.

- The building was originally constructed in 1926 as a planetarium and converted into a concert hall in the 1970s. Its **excellent acoustics** are particularly admired by performers and audiences alike.

- The Tonhalle is home to the **Düsseldorfer Symphoniker**, one of Germany's most respected orchestras, which performs both classical masterworks and contemporary compositions.

- In addition to orchestral concerts, the venue also hosts chamber music, jazz performances, film score nights, and youth-oriented concerts under programs like "Sternzeichen" and "Concert for Children."

The Tonhalle's cosmic origins are still honored in its interior lighting design, which mimics a starry sky—a magical touch that enhances the listening experience.

Theatres & Independent Venues

Beyond opera and symphonic music, Düsseldorf's performing arts scene thrives in its many theatres, cabarets, and independent venues. The city nurtures both traditional German drama and bold experimental productions.

Düsseldorfer Schauspielhaus

This is the city's largest and most important theatre for spoken drama. Designed in a striking modernist style by architect Bernhard Pfau, the Schauspielhaus is located near the Hofgarten and stages a broad program of

German and international plays, from Goethe to modern playwrights.

- The theatre is known for **literary adaptations**, contemporary social dramas, and powerful ensemble work.

- It also hosts international guest productions and often includes English-language surtitles for major shows.

Kom(m)ödchen

A historic **cabaret theatre**, Kom(m)ödchen has been a Düsseldorf institution since 1947. It blends political satire, comedy, and clever wordplay, continuing the tradition of sharp social commentary through performance.

- It was founded by Kay and Lore Lorentz, both key figures in post-war German cultural life.

- Even without fluent German, international visitors may enjoy its atmosphere and lively energy.

FFT – Forum Freies Theater

The **Forum Freies Theater** is the city's leading venue for experimental and independent performance art. It emphasizes interdisciplinary productions, dance, performance art, and socially critical themes.

- FFT showcases **emerging artists**, international guest performances, and collaborative projects that blur the lines between theatre, visual art, and activism.

- It reflects Düsseldorf's commitment to supporting **creative innovation** and offers a platform for voices often underrepresented in mainstream cultural spaces.

Other notable venues include the **Theater an der Kö** (a popular venue for comedy and boulevard theatre) and **Junges Schauspiel**, which focuses on productions for younger audiences.

Annual Events & Festivals

Düsseldorf's cultural calendar is filled with events that celebrate its diversity, history, and artistic spirit. These festivals attract both locals and international visitors, and many include free public programming.

Düsseldorf Festival! (formerly Altstadtherbst Kulturfestival)

Held each September, this multi-disciplinary festival presents theatre, dance, music, and art in both traditional and non-traditional venues.

- Known for its **bold programming**, the festival emphasizes international collaborations and site-specific performances.

- Events take place in tents, churches, warehouses, and city squares, making art accessible and surprising.

Jazz Rally Düsseldorf

Every spring, the city swings with one of Germany's largest jazz festivals. The **Jazz Rally** brings together international stars and local talent for dozens of concerts across a variety of venues.

- Genres include jazz, blues, funk, and soul.

- Many performances are held outdoors, creating a festive and relaxed atmosphere throughout the city center.

Schumannfest

Named after composer **Robert Schumann**, who lived and worked in Düsseldorf in the mid-19th century, this festival celebrates classical music with concerts, lectures, and exhibitions.

- It often includes performances by the Düsseldorfer Symphoniker and international guest ensembles.

- The program typically explores Schumann's legacy in relation to other

Romantic composers and modern interpretations of his work.

Open Source Festival

This indie and electronic music festival takes place at the **Galopprennbahn Düsseldorf** (the horse racetrack) and highlights emerging artists, DJs, and creative collectives.

- Beyond music, the festival includes a **Design Conference**, exhibitions, and talks focused on creativity and innovation.

- It is particularly popular with young audiences and showcases Düsseldorf's role in Germany's electronic music and media arts scene.

Düsseldorf's arts and performance landscape is as dynamic and varied as the city itself. From grand opera to street performance, from symphonies under the stars to underground theatre, the city pulses with a creative energy that invites visitors to see, hear, and feel more deeply. No matter when you visit, you're bound to find something on stage worth experiencing.

8. FOOD & DRINK SCENE

Düsseldorf's food and drink scene is a flavorful reflection of its history, geography, and cosmopolitan character. Nestled on the banks of the Rhine River, the city has long been a crossroads for trade and culture, resulting in a culinary landscape that blends traditional Rhineland dishes, hearty beers, and international influences. Whether you're eager to savor authentic regional specialties or explore vibrant street markets and trendy cafés, Düsseldorf offers plenty to satisfy every palate.

Traditional Cuisine & Must-Try Dishes

When visiting Düsseldorf, indulging in local cuisine is an essential part of the experience. The city and the surrounding Rhineland region have distinct culinary traditions that have been preserved and celebrated for generations.

- **Rheinischer Sauerbraten**: This marinated pot roast, typically made with beef or sometimes horse meat, is slowly braised in a tangy mixture of vinegar, spices, and sugar. It's often served with red cabbage, potato dumplings (called **Klöße**), or boiled potatoes. The dish perfectly balances sweet and sour flavors, a hallmark of Rhineland cooking.

- **Halve Hahn**: Despite the name meaning "half a chicken," this is actually a simple yet beloved sandwich consisting of a dense rye roll topped with thick slices of aged Gouda cheese, mustard, onions, and pickles. It's a classic snack often enjoyed with a glass of Altbier in the Altstadt (Old Town).

- **Himmel un Ääd** ("Heaven and Earth"): A traditional dish combining mashed potatoes (earth) and apple sauce (heaven), usually served with black pudding or fried blood sausage. This sweet and savory contrast is unique to the region and offers a taste of local culinary heritage.

- **Grilled Sausages (Bratwurst)**: You'll find numerous varieties of sausages in Düsseldorf, including the popular **Rheinische Bratwurst**. These are typically grilled over charcoal and served with mustard and freshly baked bread rolls.

- **Labskaus**: A northern German specialty that has also made its way into Düsseldorf's menus, labskaus is a hearty dish made from corned beef, potatoes, and beetroot, often accompanied by a fried egg and pickled gherkins.

Altbier Breweries & Beer Culture

Düsseldorf's beer culture is synonymous with **Altbier**, a traditional dark, top-fermented beer with a rich malt character and a slightly bitter finish. The city's Old Town boasts what is affectionately called "The Longest Bar in the World" — a dense cluster of pubs and breweries where locals and visitors alike gather to enjoy fresh Altbier straight from the tap.

- **Key Breweries**: Some of the most famous Altbier breweries include **Uerige**, **Füchschen**, **Schumacher**, and **Brauerei Im Füchschen**. Each brewery has its own distinct take on Altbier, and a visit often includes not only a pint but also hearty traditional snacks.

- **Brauhaus Experience**: Many of these breweries operate as Brauhauses (brewpubs), where you can enjoy rustic German food alongside your beer in lively, convivial settings. It's customary to drink Altbier in small 0.2-liter glasses, called **Stangen**, so you can keep your beer fresh and order multiple rounds.

- **Beer Festivals**: Düsseldorf also hosts annual beer festivals, including the popular **Japan Day Festival**, where local breweries showcase their brews alongside international fare.

Street Food & Markets: Carlsplatz, Weekly Farmers' Markets

For a more casual, fresh, and eclectic food experience, Düsseldorf's markets are the place to explore.

- **Carlsplatz Market**: The city's most famous daily market, Carlsplatz is a vibrant hub offering fresh produce, artisan cheeses, meats, baked goods, and flowers. Located near the Altstadt, the market is perfect for a leisurely stroll or grabbing a quick bite from the many food stalls selling everything from fresh oysters to Mediterranean tapas.

- **Weekly Farmers' Markets**: Scattered throughout the city on various days, farmers' markets focus on locally sourced, organic produce and regional specialties. They offer an authentic taste of Düsseldorf's agricultural surroundings, featuring seasonal fruits, vegetables, honey, bread, and homemade preserves.

- **Street Food Events**: Throughout the year, Düsseldorf hosts street food festivals where vendors from around the world come together to offer dishes ranging from Asian fusion to vegan specialties and traditional German snacks.

International Dining Options

Düsseldorf's multicultural population has infused the city's dining scene with global flavors, making it a hotspot for international cuisine.

- The **Japanese community**, one of the largest in Europe, has given Düsseldorf a well-deserved reputation as a center for

74

authentic Japanese food outside Japan. The district around Immermannstraße is filled with excellent sushi bars, ramen shops, and izakayas.

- Beyond Japanese, the city offers a rich variety of **Mediterranean restaurants** (Italian, Greek, Spanish), **Middle Eastern eateries**, and **Asian fusion spots**. You can find everything from fine dining establishments to cozy neighborhood bistros.

- For adventurous foodies, there are numerous **vegetarian and vegan restaurants** reflecting the city's growing interest in plant-based dining.

Cafés, Bakeries & Dessert Spots

No visit to Düsseldorf is complete without sampling its café culture and baked goods, which range from traditional German pastries to contemporary delicacies.

- **Cafés**: Düsseldorf has a strong café culture influenced by its proximity to France and the Low Countries. Quaint coffeehouses serve expertly brewed espresso alongside a selection of cakes and light meals. Many cafés have outdoor seating, perfect for people-watching on bustling streets.

- **Bakeries**: Traditional bakeries offer a variety of German breads, including rye, sourdough, and hearty whole grain loaves. For sweets, look for **Berliner Pfannkuchen** (German doughnuts), **Stollen** during the winter holidays, and **Apfelstrudel**.

- **Dessert Spots**: Ice cream parlors, chocolatiers, and pastry shops abound. Local specialties like **Rhenish waffles** (thin, crisp waffles often topped with powdered sugar or fruit) are a popular treat. You'll also find innovative patisseries blending classic techniques with modern flair.

Düsseldorf's food and drink scene is a rich tapestry woven from tradition and innovation, local pride, and global influence. Whether you're savoring a frothy Altbier in a centuries-old pub, shopping fresh ingredients at Carlsplatz, or enjoying fine dining with international flavors, you'll find that the city invites you to taste its unique blend of history and modernity.

9. SHOPPING IN DÜSSELDORF

Düsseldorf is not only a cultural and culinary hub but also a premier shopping destination. Known for its blend of luxury boutiques, trendy neighborhoods, and unique local crafts, the city caters to all shopping styles and budgets. Whether you are hunting for high-end designer brands, quirky vintage finds, or authentic souvenirs, Düsseldorf offers a variety of options that make shopping an experience in itself.

Luxury Shopping on Königsallee

Known locally as the **Kö**, Königsallee is Düsseldorf's iconic luxury shopping boulevard. This elegant street, lined with chestnut trees and a picturesque canal running through its center, is one of Germany's most prestigious retail destinations.

- The **Kö** hosts flagship stores for top international brands such as **Louis Vuitton**, **Gucci**, **Chanel**, and **Hermès**, alongside renowned German designers like **Joop!** and **Windsor**.

- Besides fashion, you'll find exclusive jewelers, high-end watchmakers, and luxury cosmetics boutiques.

- The street itself is as much a spectacle as the shops, with beautiful architecture and elegant cafés perfect for a stylish break between shopping.

- Königsallee's reputation extends beyond retail—it's a social hotspot where locals and visitors mingle, especially during **fashion weeks** and special shopping events.

Fun fact: The name "Königsallee" translates to "King's Avenue," originally named to reflect the street's royal elegance and prestige.

Boutiques in Flingern & Bilk

For a more independent and creative shopping experience, head to the neighborhoods of **Flingern** and **Bilk**.

- **Flingern** is known as Düsseldorf's trendsetting district, packed with small boutiques, artisan workshops, and concept stores. Here, you can discover unique clothing, handcrafted jewelry, and home décor items that blend modern design with traditional craftsmanship.

- Many stores in Flingern support local designers and sustainable fashion, making it a hotspot for eco-conscious shoppers and those looking for one-of-a-kind pieces.

- **Bilk** is another vibrant area popular with students and young creatives, offering an eclectic mix of second-hand shops, indie fashion, and art galleries.

- The weekly **Bilk Market** and occasional flea markets also provide opportunities to find vintage treasures and quirky collectibles.

Both neighborhoods have plenty of cozy cafés and bars, allowing you to relax and soak in the creative atmosphere after a day of shopping.

Vintage & Thrift Stores

Düsseldorf has a growing community of vintage and thrift store enthusiasts, reflecting a global trend toward sustainable and retro fashion.

- Vintage shops can be found scattered across the city, especially in Flingern, Bilk, and parts of the city center.

- These stores offer carefully curated selections ranging from designer vintage wear to affordable retro fashion, accessories, and even vinyl records.

- Many thrift shops also focus on sustainable fashion, encouraging recycling and upcycling.

- Popular vintage stores include **Picknweight**, where clothes are sold by weight, and **Garage**, known for its high-quality vintage designer pieces.

- For serious bargain hunters, monthly flea markets like the **Antikmarkt** (Antique Market) are perfect for finding unique antiques, old books, and rare souvenirs.

Shopping vintage in Düsseldorf not only offers style but also a fascinating glimpse into fashion history and culture.

Souvenirs & Local Products

Bringing home a piece of Düsseldorf is easy thanks to a variety of charming local products and souvenirs that reflect the city's identity and traditions.

- **Altbier Souvenirs**: Many breweries sell branded glasses, beer steins, and other memorabilia celebrating Düsseldorf's famous Altbier culture.

- **Rhenish Specialties**: You can find traditional culinary gifts such as mustard, locally produced honey, and gingerbread.

- **Handcrafted Goods**: Markets and specialty shops offer handmade ceramics, textiles, and artistic crafts made by Düsseldorf artisans.

- **Fashion Accessories**: Smaller boutiques often carry locally designed scarves, bags, and jewelry, perfect as thoughtful gifts.

- **Art Prints and Books**: For those interested in Düsseldorf's art scene, galleries and bookstores sell prints, exhibition catalogs, and photography books featuring works by local artists.

Many souvenir shops are concentrated in the **Altstadt (Old Town)**, making it convenient to combine sightseeing with souvenir shopping.

Düsseldorf's shopping scene is as diverse and dynamic as the city itself. Whether you prefer the glitz and glamour of Königsallee, the quirky charm of neighborhood boutiques, or the sustainable appeal of vintage shops, the city offers a rich and rewarding shopping experience. Take your time exploring these varied districts, and you're sure to find something special to remember your visit by.

10. NIGHTLIFE & ENTERTAINMENT

Düsseldorf's nightlife offers a vibrant blend of historic charm and modern energy, appealing to all kinds of night owls. Whether you're looking to savor a traditional Altbier in a centuries-old pub, enjoy live music in intimate venues, or dance until dawn at cutting-edge clubs, the city delivers a diverse after-dark scene that reflects its cosmopolitan spirit.

Bars & Pubs in Altstadt

The **Altstadt**, Düsseldorf's Old Town, is famously known as "The Longest Bar in the World" because of its dense concentration of bars and pubs packed into a relatively small area. This nickname reflects the area's unique atmosphere: lively, social, and steeped in tradition.

- The Altstadt is the birthplace of **Altbier**, a distinctive local dark beer with a slightly bitter taste. Many historic breweries such as **Uerige**, **Schumacher**, and **Füchschen** operate traditional pubs here where you can enjoy fresh, unfiltered Altbier straight from wooden barrels.

- These pubs often serve hearty regional snacks alongside their beer, such as **Halve Hahn** sandwiches or **Pfefferpotthast** (peppered beef stew), offering an authentic taste of Rhineland hospitality.

- The nightlife vibe ranges from cozy, rustic pubs with wooden interiors to bustling beer halls filled with locals and visitors. Evenings in the Altstadt are a social experience, often continuing well into the early morning hours.

- Many bars also feature live DJs or occasional live music, especially on weekends, contributing to a festive atmosphere.

The Altstadt is also home to a variety of cocktail bars and lounges for those seeking a more modern or sophisticated drinking experience without leaving the historic center.

Live Music Venues

Düsseldorf boasts a rich and eclectic live music scene, spanning genres from jazz and classical to indie rock and electronic.

- **Zakk**: One of the city's most important cultural venues, Zakk is renowned for its diverse programming, including live concerts, DJ sets, theatre, and art exhibitions. It attracts both local and international acts and has a reputation for supporting emerging talent and underground music scenes.

- **Jazz-Schmiede**: A staple for jazz lovers, this intimate venue features live jazz performances nearly every night, showcasing local musicians and guest artists. It's an ideal spot to experience the city's rich jazz tradition.

- **Stahlwerk**: This large concert hall hosts a wide range of music events, including rock, metal, and electronic music festivals. It is popular for big-name international tours and large-scale performances.

- **Tonhalle Düsseldorf** also hosts popular live concerts outside of its classical symphony schedule, including jazz nights and crossover projects.

Besides these, numerous smaller bars and cafés around the city offer regular live music, especially on weekends, creating a lively, grassroots musical culture.

Nightclubs & Dance Spots

For those who want to dance the night away, Düsseldorf's nightclub scene offers a mix of stylish clubs, underground venues, and multi-genre dance floors.

- The **Nachtresidenz** is one of Düsseldorf's most famous nightclubs, known for its glamorous interior and high-profile DJ line-ups. It caters to a stylish crowd looking for mainstream dance and electronic music.

- **Silq** and **Salon des Amateurs** are well-known for their focus on electronic music, including techno, house, and experimental sounds. These venues are popular among Düsseldorf's young, trend-conscious crowd and international visitors alike.

- **Club Q** offers a queer-friendly space with regular themed parties and inclusive events that celebrate diversity and creativity.

- For a more alternative vibe, clubs like **Studio 672** host indie, rock, and alternative nights, appealing to those who prefer live band performances and niche music scenes.

Düsseldorf's nightlife is generally safe and well-regulated, with most clubs closing around 4 or 5 a.m. Public transportation options make it easy to get back to your accommodation late at night.

Düsseldorf's nightlife and entertainment scene are as multifaceted as the city itself. Whether you're enjoying a quiet drink in a historic brewery, immersing yourself in live jazz, or dancing to cutting-edge electronic beats, the city offers after-dark experiences that are rich in tradition and buzzing with contemporary energy. No matter your preference, Düsseldorf ensures memorable nights filled with music, culture, and fun.

11. DAY TRIPS & NEARBY DESTINATIONS

While Düsseldorf itself offers plenty to explore, the surrounding region is filled with fascinating destinations easily reachable by train or car, making for perfect day trips. From majestic cathedrals to industrial heritage sites and unique transport experiences, these nearby cities enrich your visit with diverse cultural, historical, and recreational attractions.

Cologne: Cathedral & Cultural Sites

Just about 40 minutes away by train, **Cologne (Köln)** is a must-visit city for those interested in history, art, and architecture.

- The **Cologne Cathedral (Kölner Dom)** is the city's iconic landmark and one of

Europe's most impressive Gothic cathedrals. Its towering twin spires dominate the skyline and the interior houses stunning stained glass windows and religious relics, including the Shrine of the Three Kings.

- Beyond the cathedral, Cologne boasts numerous museums such as the **Ludwig Museum**, featuring an extensive collection of modern art including works by Picasso, and the **Roman-Germanic Museum**, showcasing artifacts from the city's Roman past.

- Cologne's charming Old Town, with its narrow cobblestone streets and lively beer halls, is perfect for wandering and sampling the local Kölsch beer.

- The vibrant **Rhine River promenade** offers scenic views and river cruises that provide a unique perspective of the city's skyline and bridges.

Cologne's blend of medieval history and contemporary culture makes it an enriching day trip from Düsseldorf.

Duisburg: Industrial Heritage & Parks

About 30 minutes from Düsseldorf by train, **Duisburg** offers a fascinating glimpse into the region's industrial past alongside modern recreational spaces.

- The **Landschaftspark Duisburg-Nord** is a former steel mill transformed into a public park that artfully combines industrial ruins with green spaces. Visitors can explore old blast furnaces, take guided tours inside industrial halls, and even go diving in a flooded gasometer.

- Duisburg is also home to the world's largest inland port, reflecting its key role in Europe's shipping and logistics network.

- The city's **Zoo Duisburg** is popular for its dolphinarium and diverse animal collections, making it a great destination for families.

- For shopping and dining, Duisburg's city center offers a variety of options from modern malls to cozy cafés.

Duisburg's blend of industrial history and nature makes it a unique and educational day trip.

Essen: Museums & Zollverein Coal Mine

Around 40 minutes from Düsseldorf by train, **Essen** is another city deeply rooted in the industrial heritage of the Ruhr region.

- The **Zollverein Coal Mine Industrial Complex** is a UNESCO World Heritage Site and a symbol of the Ruhr area's coal mining history. The site has been transformed into a cultural center with museums, art installations, and event spaces. The former coal washery is home to the **Red Dot Design Museum**, showcasing innovative industrial design.

- Essen's **Museum Folkwang** is renowned for its impressive collection of 19th and 20th-century art, including works by Van Gogh, Cézanne, and Matisse.

- The city's green spaces, such as the **Grugapark**, offer a peaceful retreat with botanical gardens, playgrounds, and seasonal festivals.

- Essen also features a thriving culinary scene with restaurants serving traditional German and international cuisine.

This mix of cultural institutions and industrial heritage makes Essen a rewarding destination for art lovers and history enthusiasts.

Wuppertal: Suspension Railway Experience

About 30 minutes northeast of Düsseldorf, **Wuppertal** is famous for its unique and historic transportation system.

- The **Wuppertal Suspension Railway (Wuppertaler Schwebebahn)** is the world's oldest electric suspended monorail, operating since 1901. It travels above the Wupper River and city streets, offering a one-of-a-kind transit experience with scenic views.

- The railway spans about 13 kilometers, connecting key parts of the city, and is still a vital means of local transport.

- Wuppertal is also known for its **Wuppertal Zoo**, extensive green parks, and vibrant arts scene, including the **Von der Heydt Museum** which features important collections of European art.

- The city has charming neighborhoods with cafés and shops, perfect for a leisurely afternoon.

Riding the suspension railway is a fun and memorable experience that highlights Wuppertal's innovative spirit.

Each of these nearby destinations offers a distinct perspective on the culture, history, and innovation of the Rhine-Ruhr region. Whether you are drawn to magnificent cathedrals, industrial landmarks turned cultural centers, or unique transport systems, these day trips provide enriching experiences that complement your stay in Düsseldorf perfectly.

12. FAMILY-FRIENDLY ACTIVITIES

Düsseldorf is a city that warmly welcomes families, offering a wide range of activities that entertain children and adults alike. From expansive parks and interactive museums to zoos and seasonal festivals, there's no shortage of family-friendly options to keep younger visitors engaged and create memorable experiences for the whole family.

Parks & Playgrounds

Düsseldorf is home to numerous parks where families can relax, play, and enjoy nature.

- **Hofgarten**: Located in the city center, the Hofgarten is Düsseldorf's oldest public park. Its wide green lawns, ponds, and walking paths provide ample space for children to run and explore. The park also has playgrounds designed for various age groups and is perfect for a family picnic.

- **Nordpark**: This park features beautifully landscaped gardens, large open spaces, and a fantastic playground area. It also houses the **Aquazoo Löbbecke Museum**, making it a great combined destination for families.

- **Rheinpark**: Along the Rhine River, Rheinpark offers walking and cycling paths, playgrounds, and scenic views of the river, ideal for a family day out.

- Numerous smaller playgrounds are scattered throughout Düsseldorf's neighborhoods, many equipped with climbing frames, swings, and sandpits.

Parks often host family-friendly events, including outdoor concerts, festivals, and seasonal activities, making them lively community hubs.

Zoos & Aquariums

Animal lovers will find several attractions that offer close encounters with wildlife.

- **Aquazoo Löbbecke Museum**: More than just an aquarium, the Aquazoo combines aquatic exhibits with natural history displays. It features over 5,000 animals, including fish, amphibians, reptiles, and insects. The museum also emphasizes conservation and education, with interactive exhibits designed to engage children in learning about biodiversity.

- **Zoo Düsseldorf**: While smaller than some major zoos, Düsseldorf's zoo is charming and family-friendly. It hosts a variety of animals, including elephants, penguins, and primates. The zoo offers educational programs and seasonal activities for children.

- Nearby, the **Wildpark Grafenberg** is a forested wildlife park where families can see deer, wild boar, and other native animals in a natural setting.

These attractions provide both fun and educational experiences that appeal to all ages.

Interactive Museums

Düsseldorf's museums cater to curious minds of all ages, with interactive exhibits and hands-on activities that make learning fun.

- **Kunstsammlung Nordrhein-Westfalen (K20 & K21)** occasionally offers family workshops and special tours tailored for children, introducing them to modern and contemporary art in engaging ways.

- The **Filmmuseum** provides insight into the history of cinema and offers family-friendly screenings and workshops.

- The **Classic Remise Düsseldorf**, an automotive center and museum, fascinates car enthusiasts with vintage vehicles and sometimes hosts events suitable for children.

- Various cultural institutions and libraries across the city regularly organize storytelling sessions, craft workshops, and educational programs designed especially for kids.

These venues help foster creativity and curiosity while keeping the whole family entertained.

Seasonal Events for Children

Throughout the year, Düsseldorf hosts numerous seasonal festivals and events that are ideal for families.

- **Christmas Markets**: During the holiday season, the city's Christmas markets transform into winter wonderlands with festive stalls, carousel rides, and special children's programs such as puppet theaters and ice skating.

- **Carnival (Karneval)**: Düsseldorf's famous Carnival is a colorful, family-friendly celebration featuring parades, costume parties, and street performances. Children often participate in special events and school celebrations.

- **Rheinwiesen Festival**: In the summer, riverside festivals often include activities for children, from face painting to craft workshops.

- **Open-Air Cinema and Theatre**: During warmer months, parks and public squares host outdoor film screenings and theatre performances suitable for families.

These seasonal events provide joyful opportunities to experience local traditions and enjoy quality family time.

Düsseldorf's family-friendly offerings ensure that visitors of all ages can find activities that excite and inspire. From playing in expansive green spaces and visiting engaging museums to enjoying festivals and animal encounters, families will find plenty to keep them entertained and create lasting memories.

13. OUTDOOR ACTIVITIES & NATURE

Düsseldorf's location along the Rhine River and its abundance of parks and green spaces make it a fantastic city for outdoor enthusiasts. Whether you prefer leisurely river cruises, scenic hiking and biking trails, or relaxing in beautifully maintained gardens, Düsseldorf offers numerous ways to enjoy nature and fresh air. Seasonal outdoor events further enhance the city's vibrant outdoor culture.

Rhine River Cruises

The Rhine River is the lifeblood of Düsseldorf, offering stunning views and a unique way to explore the city and its surroundings.

- Various companies operate **river cruises** departing from Düsseldorf's Rhine embankment. These cruises range from short sightseeing trips along the city's skyline to longer excursions that travel upriver or downriver to nearby towns.

- Cruises often feature commentary about Düsseldorf's landmarks, history, and the surrounding Rhine region, making them both relaxing and educational.

- Seasonal cruises include themed journeys such as sunset cruises, dinner cruises, and special holiday cruises during Christmas or Carnival.

- Many cruises allow passengers to combine sightseeing with dining, providing a memorable way to experience the city from the water.

Enjoying a Rhine cruise is a peaceful escape from the urban buzz, perfect for all ages and a highlight of any Düsseldorf visit.

Hiking & Biking Trails

Düsseldorf and its surrounding region boast extensive trails for hiking and biking, catering to both casual walkers and more serious cyclists.

- The **Rhine Cycle Route (EuroVelo 15)** passes through Düsseldorf, providing a scenic path along the river that connects the city to other major destinations in Germany and neighboring countries.

- Numerous local bike trails wind through parks, forests, and along the riverbanks, such as the **Kaiserswerth to Benrath route**, which combines historic sights with natural beauty.

- For hiking enthusiasts, nearby nature reserves like the **Aaper Wald** and **Rheinwiesen** offer peaceful woodland trails and open meadows.

- Bike rentals are widely available, including electric bikes, making it easy for visitors to explore at their own pace.

- Düsseldorf's flat terrain is ideal for family cycling outings and beginner-friendly hikes.

These trails not only promote an active lifestyle but also allow visitors to discover hidden corners of the city and region.

Public Parks & Gardens

Düsseldorf prides itself on its well-maintained parks and gardens, offering urban oases perfect for relaxation and recreation.

- The **Hofgarten**, located in the heart of the city, is a historic park featuring manicured lawns, fountains, and sculptures. It's popular with joggers, picnickers, and anyone seeking a green retreat.

- **Nordpark** is known for its botanical gardens and themed areas, including a Japanese garden and rose garden. It also hosts outdoor art installations and cultural events.

- The **Botanical Garden** at the University of Düsseldorf is a peaceful spot where visitors can admire diverse plant species, including exotic flora from around the world.

- The **Rheinuferpromenade** is a pedestrian-friendly riverside park with walking paths, cafés, and green spaces, perfect for strolling or sitting by the water.

- Seasonal flower displays and garden festivals are common, especially in spring and summer, adding color and vibrancy to the city's green spaces.

These parks are excellent spots to unwind, exercise, or enjoy nature within an urban setting.

Seasonal Outdoor Events

Düsseldorf's outdoor calendar is filled with seasonal events that encourage residents and visitors to enjoy the city's natural environment.

- In spring and summer, outdoor concerts, film screenings, and theatre performances are regularly held in parks and along the Rhine promenade.

- The **Rhine Festival (Rheinkirmes)**, held every summer, is one of Europe's largest funfairs, featuring rides, food stalls, fireworks, and riverside celebrations that draw large crowds.

- Autumn brings harvest festivals and open-air markets where local produce and crafts are celebrated amid colorful fall foliage.

- Winter transforms the city's squares and parks into festive Christmas markets with stalls, ice skating rinks, and holiday lights, creating a magical outdoor atmosphere.

These events showcase Düsseldorf's lively community spirit and connection to the outdoors throughout the year.

Düsseldorf's outdoor activities and natural settings offer visitors a refreshing contrast to its urban attractions. Whether cruising the Rhine, cycling scenic trails, relaxing in peaceful gardens, or joining in lively seasonal festivals, there are countless ways to enjoy the city's beautiful outdoor spaces.

14. PRACTICAL INFORMATION

Preparing for your trip to Düsseldorf involves understanding some practical details that will help you navigate the city smoothly and respectfully. This chapter covers essential language tips, connectivity, cultural customs, local laws, and emergency services, ensuring you feel confident and informed throughout your stay.

Language Tips & Common Phrases

While **German is the official language** of Düsseldorf and the rest of Germany, you'll find that **English is widely understood** in most parts of the city, especially in places frequented by international visitors—such as hotels, restaurants, museums, and public transportation hubs. However, making an effort to learn and use a few basic German expressions can greatly enhance your experience. It not only facilitates smoother communication but also demonstrates cultural sensitivity and politeness, which locals genuinely appreciate.

Even if your pronunciation isn't perfect, locals will usually be pleased that you made the effort.

Basic Greetings and Courtesies

German society places a strong emphasis on politeness and formality, particularly in initial interactions. A friendly greeting and a respectful tone go a long way.

- **Hallo** – Hello (informal and widely used)

- **Guten Morgen** – Good morning (used until late morning)

- **Guten Tag** – Good day (common from midday to early evening)

- **Guten Abend** – Good evening

- **Auf Wiedersehen** – Goodbye (formal)

- **Tschüss** – Bye (casual, friendly)

- **Gute Nacht** – Good night (used when parting at night or going to sleep)

Using these greetings appropriately helps set a friendly tone in shops, restaurants, or while asking for help.

Polite Phrases and Essentials

Politeness is fundamental in German communication. These words and expressions will help you sound respectful and courteous in all situations:

- **Bitte** – Please (also used to mean "you're welcome")

- **Danke** – Thank you

- **Vielen Dank** – Many thanks

- **Entschuldigung** – Excuse me / Sorry (used to get someone's attention or to apologize)

- **Kein Problem** – No problem

- **Gern geschehen** – You're welcome (formal, when someone thanks you)

In Germany, you may also hear the phrase **"Guten Appetit"** before meals, which means "Enjoy your meal." It's customary to say this before eating with others.

Helpful Questions and Everyday Phrases

Whether you're ordering food, shopping, or finding your way around, these practical phrases can come in handy:

- **Sprechen Sie Englisch?** – Do you speak English?

- **Ich spreche nur ein bisschen Deutsch.** – I only speak a little German.

- **Können Sie das bitte wiederholen?** – Can you please repeat that?

- **Wie viel kostet das?** – How much does it cost?

- **Wo ist die Toilette?** – Where is the bathroom?

- **Wie komme ich zum Bahnhof?** – How do I get to the train station?

- **Ich hätte gerne...** – I would like... (useful when ordering)

- **Was empfehlen Sie?** – What do you recommend?

When reading signs, you may also encounter:

- **Ausgang** – Exit

- **Eingang** – Entrance

- **Bitte nicht berühren** – Please do not touch

- **Kein Zutritt** – No entry

- **Rauchen verboten** – No smoking

Tips for Communicating Effectively

- **Speak clearly and slowly**: Even if your German is basic, clear pronunciation helps.

- **Use gestures and body language**: They can support your words and clarify meaning.

- **Download a translation app**: Useful for quick lookups or longer conversations.

- **Carry a small phrasebook**: It can be helpful when offline or in rural areas where English is less common.

In general, younger people and those in the service industry are more likely to speak English fluently, while older generations may be less confident in their English skills. Still, most people will try their best to understand

and help you, especially if you approach them politely.

Cultural Insight

Addressing someone with **"Sie"** (the formal "you") rather than **"du"** (the informal "you") is considered more respectful, especially when speaking with strangers or in formal settings. You're not expected to master all grammar rules, but being aware of this formality can leave a positive impression.

Using even a small handful of German words during your visit can lead to **warmer interactions, better service, and a deeper cultural experience.** It also reflects the spirit of international respect and curiosity that makes travel so enriching.

Electricity & Connectivity

- **Electricity:** Germany uses a 230-volt supply with a frequency of 50 Hz. The power plugs and sockets are type C and F (two round pins). If your devices have different plugs, bring a suitable adapter. Most modern electronics from North America and Asia can handle 230V, but double-check to avoid damage.

- **Internet & Mobile Connectivity:** Düsseldorf has excellent internet infrastructure. Free Wi-Fi is commonly available in hotels, cafés, shopping centers, and public libraries. Many public transport stations and major squares also offer free hotspots.

- For mobile connectivity, purchasing a local SIM card can be convenient and affordable, especially if you plan to travel around the region. Major German carriers like Telekom, Vodafone, and O2 provide good coverage.

- Public charging stations for electric vehicles are widespread, reflecting the city's commitment to sustainability.

Tipping Etiquette

Tipping in Düsseldorf is customary but not mandatory. It is appreciated as a gesture of good service and typically ranges from 5 to 10 percent of the bill.

- In restaurants and cafés, it is common to round up the bill or add a small tip when paying. For example, if your bill is €18, you might hand over €20 and say *"stimmt so"* (meaning "keep the change").

- Bartenders and taxi drivers also expect small tips, usually rounding up to the next euro or a euro or two.

- For hotel staff, a tip of 1 to 2 euros per bag for porters or housekeeping is appreciated.

- Always hand the tip directly to the person providing the service rather than leaving it on the table.

Showing appreciation with a tip is a simple way to acknowledge friendly and efficient service.

Smoking & Drinking Laws

- **Smoking:** Smoking is banned in all indoor public places in Düsseldorf, including restaurants, bars, public transport, and shopping centers. Some outdoor areas may have designated smoking zones. Always look for signs and respect non-smoking policies.

- **Drinking Age:** The legal drinking age for beer and wine is 16, while spirits and stronger alcoholic beverages can only be purchased and consumed by those aged 18 and older.

- Drinking alcohol is generally allowed in public spaces such as parks and streets unless otherwise specified by local ordinances.

- Public intoxication is discouraged, and excessive noise or disorderly behavior may attract police attention.

Following these rules helps maintain Düsseldorf's welcoming and safe environment for everyone.

Emergency Numbers & Services

Being aware of emergency contacts is essential for safety and peace of mind.

- **Emergency Phone Number (Police, Fire, Ambulance):** 112 — This number works throughout the European Union and connects you to all emergency services.

- **Police Non-Emergency:** 110 — For situations that require police assistance but are not urgent.

- **Medical Assistance:** Most hospitals have emergency rooms open 24/7. Pharmacies (*Apotheken*) are plentiful; some operate extended hours, especially on weekends.

- **Tourist Information:** Düsseldorf has several tourist information centers where you can get help, maps, and advice. They also assist with lost property and local services.

- It's advisable to have travel insurance covering health and emergencies while visiting.

Keep these numbers handy and don't hesitate to seek help if needed—emergency services in Düsseldorf are professional and efficient.

This practical information chapter ensures that your trip to Düsseldorf is safe, comfortable, and culturally respectful. With these basics covered, you'll be well-equipped to enjoy everything the city has to offer with confidence.

15. CONCLUSION & FINAL TIPS

As your journey through Düsseldorf comes to an end, we hope this guide has helped you uncover the best of what this vibrant city has to offer. From historic streets and world-class museums to lively festivals and serene parks, Düsseldorf presents a rich blend of culture, nature, and modern urban life that leaves a lasting impression on every visitor.

Reflecting on Your Trip

Traveling is not just about visiting places but experiencing them. Whether you've wandered through the bustling Altstadt, savored a refreshing Altbier in a traditional brewery, admired contemporary art, or enjoyed a peaceful walk along the Rhine promenade, Düsseldorf invites you to create your own stories and memories.

Remember that every trip is unique. Take the time to revisit your favorite spots or explore hidden gems you might have missed. Düsseldorf's charm lies in its welcoming atmosphere and the balance between history and innovation.

Final Travel Tips

- Keep your itinerary flexible to allow for spontaneous discoveries.

- Use public transport or rent a bike to experience the city like a local.

- Try local dishes and drinks to truly taste the region's culture.

- Respect local customs and regulations to ensure a smooth visit.

- Take plenty of photos and notes to share your experience with others.

We Value Your Feedback

If this guide has been helpful in planning your Düsseldorf adventure or enhancing your stay, please consider leaving a positive review on the online store where you purchased it. Your feedback not only supports the author but also helps future travelers make informed decisions.

A good review can highlight what you found most useful or enjoyable. Thank you for taking the time to share your thoughts.

Thank you for choosing this Düsseldorf Travel Guide. We wish you safe travels and many wonderful experiences on your journey ahead!

Printed in Dunstable, United Kingdom